The Case for ISO27001:2013

Second edition

The Case for ISO27001:2013

Second edition

ALAN CALDER

IT Governance Publishing

Every possible effort has been made to ensure that the information contained in this book is accurate at the time of going to press, and the publisher and the author cannot accept responsibility for any errors or omissions, however caused. Any opinions expressed in this book are those of the author, not the publisher. Websites identified are for reference only, not endorsement, and any website visits are at the reader's own risk. No responsibility for loss or damage occasioned to any person acting, or refraining from action, as a result of the material in this publication can be accepted by the publisher or the author.

Apart from any fair dealing for the purposes of research or private study, or criticism or review, as permitted under the Copyright, Designs and Patents Act 1988, this publication may only be reproduced, stored or transmitted, in any form, or by any means, with the prior permission in writing of the publisher or, in the case of reprographic reproduction, in accordance with the terms of licences issued by the Copyright Licensing Agency. Enquiries concerning reproduction outside those terms should be sent to the publisher at the following address:

IT Governance Publishing
IT Governance Limited
Unit 3, Clive Court
Bartholomew's Walk
Cambridgeshire Business Park
Ely, Cambridgeshire
CB7 4EA
United Kingdom

www.itgovernance.co.uk

First published in the United Kingdom in 2005
by IT Governance Publishing.

Second edition published in 2013.

ISBN 978-1-84928-530-8

ABOUT THE AUTHOR

Alan Calder is the founder and Executive Chairman of IT Governance Ltd (*www.itgovernance.co.uk*), an information, advice and consultancy firm that helps company boards tackle governance, risk management, compliance and information security issues. He has many years of senior management experience in the private and public sectors.

The company distributes a range of books, tools and other publications on governance, risk management, compliance and information security through its website.

ACKNOWLEDGEMENT

Some of the material in this book has appeared elsewhere in books and articles by Alan Calder; this is the first time that all the material germane to the Case for ISO27001:2013 has been gathered together in one place, re-purposed and expanded.

CONTENTS

INTRODUCTION

The replacement, in late 2005, of BS 7799-2:2002 by the international Information Security Management System Standard ISO/IEC 27001:2005 marked the beginning of the age of information security management. The update to ISO/IEC 27001 in 2013 was released to an ever-expanding information economy.

In the first eight years that BS 7799 existed as a Standard against which organisations could gain an external certification, about 1,000 were successful, worldwide. This number doubled in the subsequent 12 months. Under ISO/IEC 27001, that number has grown geometrically. This book looks at why organisations are increasingly turning to this information security management Standard.

By far the most common drivers for organisations that were successful in achieving BS 7799 'were commercial: to increase the confidence of customers, or possibly to encourage suppliers, when dealing with the organisation.'[1] By 2011, 87 percent of respondents to a BSI survey reported that implementing ISO/IEC 27001 had a positive or very positive outcome.[2]

Technology – specifically information technology – is transforming the economic and social worlds in which we work, play and live. Whether or not this is a good thing is irrelevant. The fact is that, for most people, information was stored, 20 years ago, on pieces of paper. Small numbers of

---

[1] Information Security BS 7799 Survey 2005 – Information Security Ltd.

[2] Benefits of ISO/IEC 27001 Information Security Research Report, 2011.

large mainframe computers batch-processed mundane transactions and a credit card application could take several weeks. Corporations wrote their own computer programs and avoiding GIGO (garbage in, garbage out) was the Head of IT's prime objective. Fax machines were transforming a business communication infrastructure that still depended on expensive fixed telephone lines. Information, when it existed, was hard to lay your hands on and even harder to use, manipulate or transform.

Today, 'information overload' is a commonplace complaint. Computers are ubiquitous, data is mobile, communication can be globally instantaneous and someone else can get a credit card in your name in a matter of minutes.

As we've shifted from a manufacturing to an information economy, the structure of organisational value has changed dramatically. The intangible assets (mostly intellectual capital) of most OECD organisations are now worth substantially more than their tangible assets and this trend is unlikely to reverse.

Information is the life blood of the modern business. All organisations possess and use critical or sensitive information. Roughly nine-tenths of all businesses now send e-mail across the Internet, browse the web and have a website; and 87 percent of them now identify themselves as 'highly dependent' on electronic information and the systems that process it. Information and information systems are at the heart of any organisation trying to operate in the high-speed wired world of the 21st Century.

Business rewards come from taking risks; managed, controlled risk-taking, but risk-taking nonetheless. The business environment has always been full of threats, from employees and competitors, through criminals and corporate spies, to governments and the external environment. The change in the structure of business value has led to a transformation of the business threat environment.

The proliferation of increasingly complex, sophisticated and global threats to this information and its systems, in combination with the compliance requirements of a flood of computer- and privacy-related regulation around the world, is forcing organisations to take a more joined-up view of information security. Hardware-, software- and vendor-driven solutions to individual information security challenges no longer cut the mustard. On their own, in fact, they are dangerously inadequate.

News headlines about hackers, viruses and online fraud are just the public tip of the data-insecurity iceberg. Business losses through computer failure, or major interruption to their data and operating systems, or the theft or loss of intellectual property or key business data, are more significant and more expensive.

Organisations face criminal damages, reputation loss and business failure if they fail to adequately secure their information. Directors face loss of personal reputation and time in prison if they fail in their duty to protect the information their organisations are holding.

But computer security technology, on its own, simply does not protect information. On its own, it just wastes money, gives a false sense of security and decreases business efficiency. What organisations need is a structured method for identifying the real information risks they face, the financial impact of those threats and appropriate methods of mitigating those specific, identified risks. Securing information is not rocket science, whatever the technology vendors might say. Information is at risk as much through human behaviour (and inattention) as it is through anything else. Securing information therefore requires an approach that is as much about process and individual behaviour as it is about technological defences.

And no organisation has either the time or the resources to try and work out, on its own and from first principles, how to do this effectively. Apart from anything else, the time and error profile is likely to be unattractive.

No organisation needs to. ISO27001 already exists. This Standard, which contains current information security international best practice that has already been successfully implemented in more than 20,000 organisations around the world, gives organisations a reliable and effective framework for deploying an information security management system that will preserve its assets, protect its directors and improve its competitiveness.

This book explains how.

CHAPTER 1: INFORMATION ECONOMY, INTELLECTUAL CAPITAL

Executive summary

In the information economy, businesses depend on information and a substantial proportion of their value is made of intangible and information assets. The Board has a fiduciary duty to protect and preserve these assets.

The information economy

The information, or knowledge, economy is (as we all know) fundamentally different from the old manufacturing one. Information interchange has sped up the globalisation of markets, products and resourcing. This has led to increasingly similar shopping streets selling increasingly similar products throughout the developed world. All organisations now have an online presence; for many of them, the Internet is their primary or only method of business development and communication. More than 70 percent of workers in developed economies are now knowledge, rather than manual, workers – including those factory and farm workers whose work depends on understanding and using information technology. Information networking and telecommunications connectivity make this 'global village' possible – and bring a number of specific business threats and challenges at the same time.

The key characteristics of the global information economy, in contrast to those of the older manufacturing one, are:

- Information and knowledge are not depleting resources to be protected; on the contrary, sharing knowledge drives innovation.
- Effects of location and time are diminished – virtual organisations now operate round the clock in virtual marketplaces, and organisations based on East Coast America manufacture in China, handle customer support from India and sell globally through a single website.
- Laws and taxes are difficult to apply effectively on a national basis as knowledge quickly shifts to low tax, low regulation environments.
- Knowledge-enhanced products command price premiums.
- Captured knowledge has a greater intrinsic value than 'knowledge on the hoof'.

'What's new? Simply this: Because knowledge has become the single most important factor of production, managing intellectual assets has become the single most important task of business.'[1]

Intellectual capital

Most people are aware that, for most organisations, the value of their tangible assets – land and buildings, plant and machinery, cash and so on – is different from the value of their intangible assets – the ones not carried on their books. The value of the intangible assets is usually taken, in simple terms, as being equal to the difference between the net book

---

[1] Intellectual Capital: the New Wealth of Organizations, Thomas A Stewart, 1997.

value of the business and its current market capitalisation.

In the last 20 years the apparent value of these intangible assets has grown and now, in many cases, their value exceeds that of their tangible assets – sometimes considerably. In the information age, an organisation's key asset is its intellectual capital: its human resources, retained knowledge and intangible assets. Every organisation with a long-term desire to survive and succeed in its chosen market has to focus on preserving, protecting, developing, and applying its knowledge assets – its 'intellectual capital' – for the benefit of its shareholders.

Because an organisation's intellectual capital is valuable, someone else wants it: you could argue (although most accountants might prefer not to) that the definition of an asset is that it is something valued by more than one person – after all, if no one else wants it, it's not much of an asset. If other people want what you've got, you've got to ensure they don't get it – other than on your terms. You've also got to be sure that assets which you use in your business (even if no one else knows about or wants them – yet) are protected from destruction or corruption – otherwise your business' operating capability will be hampered.

Managing this risk – preserving and protecting these assets – is a key board responsibility. Intellectual capital and information assets need to be protected so that the organisation can continue to exploit them in pursuit of its competitive strategy. Information assets depend, for their productive existence, on information and communication technology. Information security, therefore, is also (but not primarily) about computer security and system security.

ISO27001

ISO27001 is the International Standard for Information Security Management Systems and it provides organisations with best practice guidance for identifying, assessing and controlling information risks in strategic business plans and everyday operational environments. It's *the* essential Standard for the information-age organisation.

CHAPTER 2: INFORMATION, IT AND COMPETITIVENESS

Executive summary

Information security is essential if your organisation's productivity and competitive position is to be protected.

Academic research

Academic research[1] largely confirms the view that the growth in Western economies since 1995 can largely be linked to the deployment and use of information technology. Studies, and experience, suggest that – excepting the slowdown in the mid-2000s – this growth is sustainable.

Other studies[2], examining and comparing specific industries (e.g. finance and manufacturing), concluded that there are circumstances where further IT investment will not provide competitive advantage over other firms in the sector, but that investment is nevertheless essential just to stay in the race.

Productivity improvements and competitive edge are the two overwhelming reasons for pursuing IT investment. No

---

[1] *See (for instance):* 'Is the Information Technology Revolution Over?' (*www.federalreserve.gov/pubs/feds/2013/201336/index.html*), published by the Board of Governors of the Federal Reserve System (US), March 2013.

[2] *See (for instance):* 'Information and Communications Technology as a General Purpose Technology: Evidence from U.S. Industry Data' (*www.frbsf.org/economic-research/publications/economic-review/2008/er1-15.pdf*), FRBSF Economic Review 2008.

board invests in IT because it's fun: the investment has to pay off – even if it only pays off in terms of keeping up with the competition.

It is also clearly the case that there are many new, innovative businesses identifying new ways of deploying information technology, creating new business models that are already destroying many existing businesses. Of course, not all of the new business models will survive but some, like Amazon for instance, force a whole sector to redefine how it does business.

Competitive environment

Survival and success in today's business environment requires inventiveness and adaptation; Bill Gates always said: 'Microsoft is never more than two years away from failure.' You have to innovate, find new markets and products, new ways of adding value. You also have to execute current strategies flawlessly just to make sure you're still in with a chance at the new ones.

And flawless execution, in the information economy, depends on the productivity and effectiveness of your human capital, your staff. You have to simplify their working environment, remove problems and barriers, and give them the information and information technology tools they need. In the same way that you want any new computer systems to be capable of interacting with the old so that information doesn't have to be transferred laboriously from one to the other, you should also want new computer systems to work smoothly and efficiently: no data losses, no corruption, no downtime.

And that means that information security ought to be built

into your information system's infrastructure from the outset. In order for your people to work productively and effectively with information, they need to be able to get at it, it needs to be there and it needs to be safe. This means that your default information system security setting ought to be: information availability is preserved (no viruses, no attacker-created system or computer downtime, no data destruction, whether deliberate or accidental), as is its confidentiality (no exposure of information to people who shouldn't see it) and its integrity (no data corruption, whether deliberate or accidental).

Software is imperfect (but industrial machinery also broke down); it has vulnerabilities that can be exploited or which can cause problems. The speed with which hardware and software evolves means that we are unlikely to stand still long enough for any one hardware and software platform to become completely secure and stable – because, by the time it was, everyone would have moved on to using a more up-to-date (although less secure) alternative.

It simply makes sense for any competitive business to take appropriate steps to ensure that its valuable knowledge workers can use its information technology infrastructure without fear or hindrance. Technology should be ubiquitous and safe. ISO27001 enables you to achieve that.

ISO27001

In the unsafe information economy, ISO27001 goes one step further. It tells your potential customers, employees and partners that your information systems are safe and secure – to a recognisable, externally audited, international standard – that yours is an environment in which they will be able to work productively and efficiently, and, because you have proved that you can be trusted with information, that your organisation is good to do business with. Information security and reputation go hand in hand.

CHAPTER 3: INFORMATION THREATS

Executive summary

All organisations possess information, or data, that is either critical or sensitive. This information is a substantial component of the organisation's intellectual capital. Information is widely regarded as the lifeblood of modern business. More than 90 percent of businesses now identify themselves as 'highly dependent' on electronic information and the systems that process it. This information faces a range of threats, some simple, some complex, and all with the potential to significantly damage an organisation.

Threats

'Cyber threat' is now the most widely used term to describe threats in the digital world. As in the analogue one, cyber threats originate with people. These people fall into five groups:

- Criminals (thieves, fraudsters, serious organised crime).
- Malefactors (hackers, vandals, terrorists, cyber warriors, some ex-employees and other disgruntled or vengeful individuals).
- Spies (commercial and governmental).
- Undesirables (scam artists, spammers, 'ethical' hackers and nerds).
- The incompetent, or the simply unaware (staff, contractors, customers and other third parties).

From an organisational perspective, these people are found both inside and outside the organisation (the balance overall is probably 50:50). There are a substantial number of people in each category and, because of the nature of the information economy, they are able to exert an influence out of proportion to their numbers.

The digital threats, and the type of attacks that express them, have the same sort of objectives as they do in the analogue world, but because of the nature of computers, digital data and the Internet, their characteristics are different. These characteristics were originally identified by Bruce Schneier[1] as:

- Automation: computers automate mundane tasks; illegal or destructive activity with which someone would struggle to cost-effectively achieve critical mass in the analogue world can be automated. Computers make Denial of Service attacks and large-scale junk mail possible, just as they enable 100 percent surveillance of the Internet communications traffic of any individual or organisation.
- Data collection: digital data requires less storage space than the equivalent analogue information and can be more quickly harvested, stored and mined. What can be done will (often) be done and, as a result, massive databases of personal and commercial data now exist all over the world. They make spamming, surveillance and identity theft that much easier.
- Action at a distance: in cyber space, the bad guys are just a mouse click away; the criminal who is targeting your network may be based in Chechnya, Moldavia or on a Pacific island. He will be just as effective, quick

---

[1] *Secrets and Lies: Digital Security in a Networked World,* Bruce Schneier, 2004.

and silent as a criminal down the road, far harder to trace and arrest than his analogue equivalent, and financially more successful.

- Propagation: the Web enables ideas, skills and digital tools to be shared around the world within hours. It also enables techniques to be widely replicated and a vast array of computers to be linked into any one attack.

Attack categories

The types of attacks that occur in cyber space are:

- Criminal attacks (fraud, theft and grand larceny, identity theft, hacking, extortion, phishing, IPR and copyright theft, piracy, brand theft, 'spoofing').
- Destructive attacks (cyber terrorism, hackers, ex-employees, vengeful individuals, cyber war, cyber vandals, anarchists, viruses).
- Nerd attacks (Denial of Service attacks, publicity hounds, adware).
- Espionage attacks (data and IPR theft, spyware).

These attacks affect businesses indiscriminately. Well-understood software flaws (called 'vulnerabilities', by both the 'ethical' and unethical sides of the hacking industry) are widely distributed through an increasingly always-on Internet of ill-defended computers. Individual businesses are rarely directly or individually targeted in an attack (unless they have very substantial assets or some other significant value to the attacker), but they are nevertheless at risk in an environment where automation, action at a distance and propagation enable an attacker to successfully target a very big number of smaller fish. Why target one computer when you can target them all?

Malefactors know that the majority of smaller businesses have inadequate cyber protection and they exploit this, for instance commandeering large numbers of unprotected computers in huge zombie networks, to mount large-scale attacks on targets, usually for purposes of extortion and to distribute floods of spam. Increasingly, small organisations are digitally infiltrated in order to ensure that spear phishing attacks are undetectable. Defences need to be proportionate.

Large businesses and public-sector organisations, which have significant assets to protect or which make attractive, high-profile targets, are directly threatened. Their networks are more extensive and more complex, and the quantity and diversity of people and organisations involved with them is so great that they have to be very systematic in identifying and responding to the more significant threats they face.

ISO27001

The Standard provides guidance on identifying and assessing threats. Not all threats are likely to occur and, for those that are, it is essential to have appropriate defences in place. Appropriate defences can be the difference between success and failure, between survival and collapse.

CHAPTER 4: INSECURITY IMPACTS

Executive summary

No organisation is immune to the complex range of threats to its information assets and technology infrastructure. The financial, reputational, operational and punitive impacts of successful cyber attacks or information security failures are significant.

Types of impact

'Impact' is the consequence of the realisation of a threat. It is usually quantified financially, in terms of the likely loss to the organisation. Estimation of likely loss is inexact, but should take into account both direct and indirect costs, including the likely business cost of reputational damage, loss of business, remedial advertising, investigating, closing the stable door and so on:

- Every organisation will suffer multiple instances of the abuses and attacks identified in this book.
- Business activity will be disrupted. Downtime in business-critical systems (such as ERP systems) can be catastrophic for an organisation. However quickly service is restored, there will be an unwanted and unnecessary cost in doing so. At other times, lost data may have to be painstakingly reconstructed and, sometimes, it will be lost forever.
- Privacy will be violated. Organisations have to protect the personal information of employees and customers. If this privacy is violated, there may – under data

protection and privacy legislation – be legal action, penalties and substantial restitutionary cost.

- Organisations will suffer direct financial loss. Protection in particular of commercial information and customers' credit card details is essential. Loss or theft of commercial information, ranging from business plans and customer contracts, to intellectual property, product designs and industrial know-how, can all cause long-term financial damage to the victim organisation. Computer fraud, conducted by staff with or without third-party involvement, has an immediate direct financial impact.
- Reputations will be damaged. Organisations that are unable to protect the privacy of information about staff and customers, and which consequently attract penalties and fines, will find their corporate credibility and business relationships severely damaged and their expensively developed brand and brand image dented.
- The reputations of directors will be tarnished and, in extreme cases, board members will face personal fines and imprisonment.

Organisations in a number of important surveys[1] are now significantly more pessimistic about the future outlook for information security breaches, believing that incidents will happen more often in future and be harder to detect. However:

- While almost all large businesses have an established information security policy, half of all small businesses

---

[1] E.g. The UK Department for Business, Innovation and Skills' Information Security Breaches Survey 2013 and the Ernst & Young Global Information Security Survey 2012.

do not.
- Processes for keeping anti-virus software up to date are often weak.

As a result, security breaches continue to cost industry worldwide many billions of pounds every year. The fact that half of all businesses are still spending 5 percent or less of their IT budget on security – and, consequently, suffering losses significantly in excess of the likely cost of defending against them – reflects severe information security governance inadequacies.

ISO27001

Deployment of an ISMS developed in line with the international Standard of information security best practice is the fundamental step towards effective information security governance, and pays off handsomely in terms of losses averted.

CHAPTER 5: 'TRADITIONAL' THREATS

Executive summary

All organisations face a range of threats that have been around – and getting progressively worse – for a number of years. Few organisations have taken adequate steps to deal with them. Even as far back as 2001, the CBI Cyber crime Survey recognised that 'deployment of technologies such as firewalls may provide false levels of comfort unless organisations have performed a formal risk analysis and configured firewalls and security mechanisms to reflect their overall risk strategy.'

Unless the organisation actually has a risk strategy, it's not going to be able to ensure that its cyber defences will meet its requirements.

Viruses and hackers

Viruses and hackers represent a particular threat to information security. They can be highly advanced, dedicated and persistent, and no single defence on its own can protect you from them:

- Unisys reported in 2010 that a single crimeware kit – called 'Zeus' – had infected almost 90 percent of all Fortune 500 companies. Zeus is able to penetrate almost 55 percent of systems protected with anti-malware software.[1]

---

[1] Zeus Malware: Threat Banking Industry (*http://botnetlegalnotice.com/citadel/files/Guerrino_Decl_Ex1.pdf*), published by Unisys, May 2010.

- Akamai reports that the number of DDOS attacks in the fourth quarter of 2012 was up 200 percent over 2011[2].

Hackers (black hat, white hat and grey hat), crackers, script kiddies and automated hacking exploits all mean that no computer, no network and no information asset anywhere in the world is safe. Any computer that connects to the Internet will be 'fingered' by an automated 'sniffer' and 'brute force' or 'dictionary' attacks can, in minutes, run through every word in the dictionary looking for the password.

There are more than one million known viruses 'in the wild', with the number increasing daily. Viruses, worms and Trojans propagate globally in minutes and the gap between identification of a software vulnerability and release of the first related exploit has fallen to less than a day – the 'zero day exploit'. Worms and Trojans are ever more virulent; the installation of anti-virus software is not, of itself, an adequate defence. Malware that attacks mobile devices, the emerging malware issue of 2012/13, is still outside the scope of many anti-virus software packages.

Spam

Spam continues to consume bandwidth and, as spam technology becomes more sophisticated, so spam filtering technology needs to keep pace. With spam reportedly at about 85 percent of all e-mail, and the fact that one man's spam is another's useful new product information, organisations need an intelligent solution to the challenge

---

[2] 'DDOS Attacks Growing: but How Much?'
(*www.esecurityplanet.com/network-security/ddos-attacks-growing-but-how-much.html*), published by eSecurity Planet, April 2013.

that protects their resources without disabling their businesses.

Commercial espionage

As recent whistle-blowers have shown, every major intelligence organisation in the world devotes substantial resources to both political and strategic commercial espionage. The theft of product and marketing information, of contractual and negotiating position intelligence, can dramatically alter the balance in a complex negotiation – and the impact on a smaller company can be even more destructive than on a larger one.

Insider threats

An *Infosecurity* survey found that: 'more than half of all security incidents (58%) can be attributed to the wider insider family'[3]

These internal security incidents included the introduction of viruses or other malware via mobile devices at 82 percent, and – alarmingly – inadvertent human error at 87 percent.

Fraud

Fraud is the most debilitating and destructive of insider security threats and the financial controls that evolved to protect organisations against insider fraud in the pre-digital

---

[3] '58% Information Security Incidents Attributed to Insider Threat' (*www.infosecurity-magazine.com/view/32222/58-information-security-incidents-attributed-to-insider-threat-/*), published by Infosecurity Magazine, May 2013.

age are inadequate in the digital one. It is essential that internal control structures evolve rapidly so that disasters of the type that destroyed Enron, Arthur Andersen and Barings can be avoided.

Financial organisations and quoted companies already face significant restrictions on the type (and timing) of information that can be published; modern technology – mobile phones, tablets, MP3 players, USB sticks, Instant Messaging, social media – are capable of outflanking 'traditional' security controls.

Staff

Malicious staff are a key source of information threat. Staff, contractors and subcontractors who wish to damage an organisation can usually do so with impunity, particularly where information security controls are weak and they have adequate access privileges – through, for instance, a system administrator password, a covert channel, or an inadequately partitioned network. Of course, the point of greatest danger is usually after someone has decided to leave, but hasn't yet resigned; the fact that so few organisations have an adequate process for managing information access rights for exiting employees is a root cause of the level of insider destruction to information systems.

Systems failures

Systems failure – whether through incompetence, 'fat fingers' or unpredicted external act – can be enough to severely disrupt or destroy any business. Few organisations have adequate, adequately tested, business continuity or disaster recovery plans. Few organisations, as a result, are able to survive a severe disruption, and this simple governance failure can have an incalculable impact on shareholders, employees, customers and suppliers.

ISO27001

The first stage in the deployment of an ISO27001 Information Security Management System (ISMS) is the identification and assessment of the threats that might impact the organisation, and a prioritisation of them based on their likelihood and potential harm they might cause. Risk assessment ensures that risks are appropriately addressed.

CHAPTER 6: INFORMATION RISK IN LARGE ORGANISATIONS

Executive summary

The information security risks and regulatory pressures faced by larger organisations are of a different league to those faced by smaller ones. Both the threats and the vulnerabilities are significantly different and, as a result, larger organisations suffer more security incidents than the average: ISBS 2013[1], for instance, reported that 93 percent of large companies had experienced an information security breach, compared to an overall rate of 87 percent.

Threats to larger organisations

The threats, both external and internal, are more significant, and this reflects the perceived depth, quantity and value of the larger organisation's information assets, its reputation and profile, and the number of people interested in targeting it. The 2013 ISBS showed that 91 percent of larger organisations had suffered one or more malicious incidents, compared to an overall figure of 76 percent. Threats range from hackers through cyber criminals, organised crime and activists of one sort or another to spies and cyber terrorists – all depending on the organisation.

Each sector has its own niche criminals: phishers target

---

[1] '2013 Information Security Breaches Survey'
(*www.pwc.co.uk/assets/pdf/cyber-security-2013-technical-report.pdf*),
published by PwC and the Department for Business, Innovation and Skills, 2013.

consumer financial services companies; industrial spies target intellectual property companies; activists target those companies they perceive as having an environmental or social impact of which they disapprove; hackers target those companies whose scalp will bring them the most prestige; and cyber terrorists target those companies through which they think they can inflict the most damage on the West. Fraudsters target any organisations where they can find a way of siphoning off cash, and probably work from inside.

More people are made redundant by, or fall out with, large organisations, and more contractors have their contracts terminated by large organisations – not proportionally, but in absolute terms, and simply because such large numbers of people are employed by any large organisation. There are, therefore, likely to be many more people with a grudge against any one larger organisation than there are against any smaller one.

Information leaked by a larger company is likely to be more price sensitive than that about a smaller one; details of its strategic plans (including mergers, acquisitions, restructurings, product launches, logistics, procurement, trial results and so on) are likely to have substantially more cash value than similar information from much smaller companies, and insiders are therefore more likely to be tempted to try to profit from such privileged information.

And, of course, for regulators and enforcers, targeting one or two non-compliant larger businesses brings a better return on investment than pursuing a number of smaller ones while, for institutional shareholders, the expectation is that larger organisations will be models of transparent, effective corporate governance and compliance.

Vulnerabilities in larger organisations

Paradoxically, larger organisations often have more vulnerabilities than smaller ones:

- Almost all larger organisations have now gone digital: e-mail, employee Internet access and transactional websites are standard; wireless networking and remote access are being rapidly deployed.
- Larger organisations are more complex: they have multiple divisions and business units (each with its own management and operational ethos, each with sufficient local discretion to take actions that will seriously compromise the parent organisation) operating internationally and across multiple jurisdictions, with different products and services and, therefore, different information technology needs.
- Large organisations have often been built through a number of acquisitions, each of which brought a slightly different information technology infrastructure (architecture, hardware, operating systems, applications, bespoke software, working practices, culture, values and philosophy) to the party, not all of which has yet been (or is intended to be) successfully integrated into a single, harmonious whole.
- While every system has its own vulnerabilities, the complexity of the whole creates another series of super-vulnerabilities. Most large organisations also have one or more legacy systems, which individual units or divisions may depend on, and which are no longer capable of integration into the overall

architecture and may no longer be supported by their vendors. They work, though, for the moment.

- Their multiple suppliers and volumes of customers all want electronic linkages with the company, and every such linkage is also a point of vulnerability.
- Larger companies are more likely to have outsourced significant parts of their operations; every outsourcing contract is a potential vulnerability.
- There are more people working in larger organisations; this means that there are more opportunities for someone to err, and for that error to have a negative impact on the availability, confidentiality or integrity of the organisation's information assets. The 2013 ISBS, for instance, identified the fact that 66 percent of large organisations had experienced an accidental systems failure and data corruption, compared to a rate of 59 percent for small businesses.

Impacts on larger organisations

The impacts on larger businesses are significantly worse than for small businesses. According to ISBS 2013, percentages of large organisations, compared to small organisations, for each of the following, was:

- Virus infection and software disruption: 41 percent against 40 percent
- Unauthorised access to systems or data by staff: 66 percent against 35 percent
- External intrusions into systems: 78 percent against 60 percent
- Computer-related theft or fraud: 16 percent against 12 percent

- The total cost of the worst incident, in a larger company, was between £450k and £850k, compared to a range of £35k to £65k overall.

Data protection and privacy regulation in larger organisations

Complex organisations, with diversified or (partially) virtual business models, operating in and across a number of legal jurisdictions, also have a more complex regulatory compliance task than smaller ones. While any one regulation (and its related compliance failure) might apply only to a subsidiary national entity, it is the global parent whose reputation is damaged. The more failures, the more damage; in a global marketplace, where information travels at the 'speed of light', such failures can have a dramatically destructive effect. Moreover, it's the larger organisations that are targeted by data thieves and by regulatory 'enforcers' looking for a scalp; smaller ones have less valuable information to steal, and prosecuting them doesn't win headlines or advance a career.

ISO27001

Clearly, information security and information regulatory compliance is an even more serious undertaking for larger organisations than for smaller ones. ISO27001 provides a structured framework and best practice guidance that helps any large organisation tackle the issues in a structured and comprehensive fashion that will demonstrate, to any court, clear intent to meet regulatory compliance requirements.

CHAPTER 7: ORGANISED CRIME

Executive summary

Organised crime has taken to the Internet in a big way. Cyber crime forms a significant ongoing risk for all organisations: if it is worth taking action to secure premises, it is even more worthwhile to secure digital business areas.

Impacts of organised crime

A Detica report, in conjunction with the UK's Office of Cyber Security and Information Assurance, estimated that the cost of cyber crime in the UK had reached £27bn per annum by 2011.[1] By way of contrast, a 2001 global study by the UK DTI found that lapses in security policy had cost European businesses alone more than £4.3 billion in that year due to Internet-related crime.

PricewaterhouseCoopers' Global Economic Crime Survey 2011[2] questioned 3,877 organisations in both the public and private sectors. 48 percent of them are reported to have said that 'they perceive the risk of cyber crime to be on the rise'. In their 2013 US State of Cybercrime Survey[3],

---

[1] The Cost of Cyber Crime (*www.gov.uk/government/uploads/system/uploads/attachment_data/file/60943/the-cost-of-cyber-crime-full-report.pdf*), published by Detica Ltd, 2011.
[2] Cybercrime: Protecting against the growing threat (*www.pwc.com/en_GX/gx/economic-crime-survey/assets/GECS_GLOBAL_REPORT.pdf*), published by PwC, November 2011.
[3] Key findings from the 2013 US State of Cybercrime Survey (*www.pwc.com/en_US/us/increasing-it-effectiveness/publications/assets/us-state-of-cybercrime.pdf*), published by PwC, June 2013.

7. Organised Crime

PricewaterhouseCoopers showed that more than a third of electronic crimes were caused by insiders. Despite this prevalence, only half of all companies surveyed stated that they had a formalised plan for responding to information security threats originating from within the organisation.

Europol, the European Police agency, observed in its 2011 report on EU organised crime: 'a significant expansion in cyber crime [is anticipated], particularly Internet facilitated theft of personal and financial data.' The report also observes that 'Misuse by criminal groups particularly of the Internet to commit a range of offences, and financial transfer systems to launder illicit proceeds, highlights the truly global nature of some horizontal crime problems, and the extent to which the distinction between the internal and external security of the EU has already been blurred.'[4]

The Computer Security Institute (CSI), with the participation of the San Francisco Federal Bureau of Investigation's Computer Intrusion Squad, has now conducted 15 annual surveys[5] into information security at the CSI member firms. The results of the most recent survey showed that in 2011 individual financial losses to criminal abuse, across the 351 reached as high as $25 million. While this was a remarkable outlier, and is not representative of the median, close to half of all respondents reported having been the subject of a direct criminal attack. By far the most common form of attack came from malware (67.1 percent), while phishing scams (38.9 percent) and laptop/mobile device theft (33.5 percent)

[4] EU Organised Crime Threat Assessment (www.europol.europa.eu/sites/default/files/publications/octa_2011_1.pdf), published by Europol, 2011.
[5] CSI Computer Crime and Security Survey 2010/2011 (gocsi.com/survey), published by CSI, 2011.

also represent significant threats to the organisation. It was clear that nearly 80 percent of those who took part in the overall survey were unable (because they had no method of tracking) or unwilling (because of the possible reputational damage) to provide estimates of their financial losses from the successful attacks they had experienced. Equally clear is the fact that incidents of cyber crime originate equally from outside and inside the attacked computer systems.

The conclusions of the Confederation of British Industry's (CBI) 2001 Cybercrime Survey[6], which polled 154 member firms and found that two-thirds of them had suffered serious computer crime in the previous 12 months, are even more valid more than a decade later. Nearly 60 percent predicted that cyber crime would become even more of a problem in the future. The Director-General of the CBI, Sir Digby Jones, was quoted as saying, 'Fears about potential losses and damage to reputation from cybercrime are stalling the growth of e-business, especially for B2B transactions. That growth will only come when all parties are reassured that adequate security is in place to protect them.'

'Over its seven-year lifespan', CSI concluded in 2004, 'the survey has told a compelling story. A sense of the 'facts on the ground' has emerged. There is much more illegal and unauthorised activity occurring in cyber space than corporations admit to their clients, stockholders and business partners or report to law enforcement. Incidents are widespread, costly and commonplace.'

---

[6] Cybercrime Survey 2001: Making the Information Superhighway Safe for Business, Published by the Confederation of British Industry, August 2001.

ISO27001

While deployment of an ISO27001 ISMS will not stop all criminal activity, it will reduce the instances of criminality inside the organisation while increasing the prospects of early identification of crime and a rapid, controlled response that minimises damages and loss.

CHAPTER 8: TERRORISM

Executive summary

Cyber crime is a serious issue. It may be a lesser danger to organisations than the effects of what is called 'cyber war': cyber war is even less discriminate than criminal activity, but potentially more devastating. Every organisation has a role to play in securing cyber space against terrorist attacks.

Cyber-capabilities

In 2009, the US President announced that, 'America's economic prosperity in the 21st Century will depend on cybersecurity.'[1] This statement was supported by the US General Accounting Office (GAO) in a report on cyber security in February 2013, stating, 'The evolving array of cyber-based threats facing the nation pose threats to national security, commerce and intellectual property, and individuals.'
The UK's 2012 National Security Strategy identified cyber attack as one of the four highest-priority risks faced by the UK. In recent years we have seen evidence of the severity of threat in a series of highly advanced attacks. An advanced persistent threat posed by organised crime and state-level entities, with attacks against enterprises such as Google, Coca-Cola, NASA and Lockheed Martin; Operation Aurora was a series of attacks on large US companies beginning in 2009, and ascribed to China; in

---

[1] President Barack Obama, 'Remarks by the President on Securing Our Nation's Cyber Infrastructure', 29 May 2009.

2007, there were attacks on Estonia's critical national infrastructure; malware such as Stuxnet, Duqu and Flame all demonstrate that an international military crisis is also likely to be accompanied by a cyber attack.

Any response to a major national incident also depends on information stored in electronic information systems. This makes the threat of cyber attacks doubly dangerous, as the response to the assault can be compromised by the attack itself. Every significant terrorist or criminal organisation is believed to have cyber-capabilities and to have become very sophisticated in its ability to plan and execute attacks using the most recent technology.

Eliza Manningham-Butler, Director General of the UK's Security Service, said this at the 2004 CBI annual conference: 'A narrow definition of corporate security including the threats of crime and fraud should be widened to include terrorism and the threat of electronic attack. In the same way that health and safety and compliance have become part of the business agenda, so should a broad understanding of security, and considering it should be an integral and permanent part of your planning and Statements of Internal Control; do not allow it to be left to specialists. Ask them to report to you what they are doing to identify and protect your key assets, including your people.'

More than 900 million computers are linked to the Internet; many of them are vulnerable to indiscriminate cyber attack. The critical infrastructure of the first world is subject to the threat of cyber assaults, ranging from defacing websites to undermining critical national computer systems. In February 2003, the White House published the *National*

Strategy to Secure Cyberspace[2], in which the President recognised that securing cyber space would be an extraordinarily difficult task, requiring the combined and coordinated effort of the whole of society and that, without such an effort, an infrastructure that is 'essential to our economy, security and way of life' could be disrupted to the 'extent that society would be debilitated'.

ISO27001

Every organisation has a role to play in society's survival of a terrorist attack, which is to take its own precautions to ensure that it has a reasonable prospect of survival. The Standard provides guidelines that, when deployed, reduce the organisation's level of exposure to the impacts of terrorist attacks while improving its own business continuity arrangements.

---

[2] The National Strategy to Secure Cyberspace (*www.us-cert.gov/sites/default/files/publications/cyberspace_strategy.pdf*), published by US-CERT, August 2003.

CHAPTER 9: EVOLVING THREAT ENVIRONMENT

Executive summary

The current situation is not good, and is unlikely to get better. All boards need to take action to deal with current risks; they also need to ensure that they are able to cope with future ones.

Key trends

A number of significant trends mean that information security will become even more challenging in the years ahead:

- The use of distributed computing is increasing. Computing power has migrated from centralised mainframe computers and data processing centres to a distributed network of desktop, laptop and micro computers, and this makes information security much more difficult.
- Cloud computing has expanded massively throughout the business world, providing small businesses with what would otherwise be unaffordable computing power. This, however, places the security of your information in another organisation's hands and demands stringent controls on the connection to these services.
- There is a strong trend towards mobile computing. The use of laptop computers, tablets, mobile phones, digital cameras, portable projectors and MP3 players has made

working from home or on the road relatively straightforward, with the result that network perimeters are becoming increasingly porous. There are many more remote access points to networks, and the fast-growing number of easily accessible endpoint devices increases the opportunities to break into networks and steal or corrupt information.

- There has been a dramatic growth in the use of the Internet for business communication, underpinning the development of Instant Messaging, social media, wireless, VoIP and broadband. The Internet provides an effective, immediate and powerful method for organisations to communicate on all sorts of issues. This exposes all these organisations to the security risks that go with connection to an unregulated environment and deployment, in an enterprise setting, of tools originally designed for consumers – and which have little or no enterprise-strength security capability.

- Better hacker tools are available every day, on hacker websites that, themselves, proliferate. These tools are improved regularly and fewer and fewer technologically proficient criminals – and computer literate terrorists – are enabled to cause more and more damage to target networks.

- Hacking as a Service and Fraud as a Service make criminal activity even easier; hacking training for 'newbies' is also widely available on the Internet. Secure browsers and the DarkNet help criminals hide their activities from justice.

- Increasingly, hackers, virus writers and spam operators are cooperating to find ways of spreading more spam: not just because it's fun, but because direct e-mail marketing of dodgy products is highly lucrative.

Phishing, spear phishing, pharming and other Internet fraud activity has continued evolving and will become an ever greater problem.

- This will lead, inevitably, to an increase in blended threats that can only be countered with a more effective combination of technologies and processes.
- Increasingly sophisticated technology defences, particularly around user authorisation and authentication, will drive an increase in social-engineering-derived hacker attacks.

ISO27001

In an increasingly threatening environment, directors need to take appropriate action to deal with risks to their business from threats to their information and technology assets and infrastructure. They don't have time to re-invent the wheel, to solve the security problems afresh at every organisation, nor do they need to. Information insecurity is a common problem and a common, best-practice solution has emerged: ISO27001 provides a vendor-independent, system-agnostic information security framework that any organisation, anywhere in the world, can apply to help manage its information-related risks.

CHAPTER 10: REGULATORY COMPLIANCE

Executive Summary

Today's regulatory environment is increasingly complex, the penalties for failure unattractive and the route to effective compliance not clear. ISO27001 provides a best-practice solution to the range of regulatory issues faced by directors.

The regulatory conundrum

Organisations have traditionally responded to regulatory compliance requirements on a law-by-law, or department-by-department basis. That was, last century, a perfectly adequate response. There were relatively few laws, compliance requirements were generally firmly established and well understood, and the jurisdictions within which businesses operated were well defined.

In the 21st Century, all that has changed. Rapid globalisation, increasingly pervasive information technology, the evolving business risk and threat environment, and today's governance expectations have, between them, created a fast-growing and complex body of laws and regulations – such as data protection and privacy legislation (e.g. HIPAA, GLBA, DPA) and governance requirements (e.g. SOX and Turnbull) – that all impact the organisation's IT systems. While global companies are at the forefront of finding effective compliance solutions, every organisation, however small, and in whatever industry, is faced with the same broad range of regulatory requirements.

These regulatory requirements focus on the confidentiality, integrity and availability of electronically held information, and primarily – but not exclusively – on personal data. Many of the new laws appear to overlap and, not only is there very little established legal guidance as to what constitutes compliance, new laws and regulatory requirements continue to emerge. Increasingly, these laws have a geographic reach that extends to organisations based and operating outside the apparent jurisdiction of the legislative or regulatory body that originated them.

Regulatory requirements in all these areas concentrate on preserving the confidentiality, integrity and availability of electronic data held by organisations operating within the sector. Regulations, which are technology-neutral, describe what must be done, but not how. Organisations are left to establish, for themselves, how to meet these requirements.

In most instances, there is not yet a body of tested case law and proven compliance methodologies to which organisations can turn in order to calibrate their efforts. There are no technology products that, of themselves, can render an organisation compliant with any of the data security regulations, because all data security controls consist of a combination of technology, procedure and human behaviour. In other words, installing a firewall will not protect an organisation if there are no procedures for correctly configuring and maintaining it, and if users habitually bypass it (through, for instance, Instant Messenger, Internet browsing or the deployment of rogue wireless access points).

In the face of new, blended, complex and evolving threats

to their data, organisations have business and regulatory obligations to protect, maintain and make that data available when it is required. They have to do this in an uncertain compliance environment where the rewards for success don't grab headlines, but the penalties for failure do. Fines, reputation and brand damage and, in some circumstances, time in prison for directors are outcomes that every business wants to avoid, and wants to avoid as systematically and cost-effectively as possible.

The adoption of an externally validated, best-practice approach for information security – one that provides a single, coherent framework which enables simultaneous compliance with multiple regulatory requirements – is, therefore, a solution to which organisations are increasingly turning.

ISO27001

ISO27001 provides just such a solution. It focuses on the confidentiality, availability and integrity of data and its key precepts and requirements all occur in the regulatory requirements. Implementation of an ISO27001 framework enables an organisation to comply, at one step (and subject to specific documentation and working practices tailored for each individual regulation), with all the core requirements of information-related regulation anywhere in the world.

CHAPTER 11: DATA PROTECTION AND PRIVACY

Executive summary

Privacy and data protection are linked business issues that are now a global business imperative. Failure to comply with privacy and data protection regulations can have expensive commercial and punitive consequences.

There are also good business reasons for protecting personal privacy. A successful business in the information economy depends on users having confidence in the confidentiality, availability and integrity of electronic information and communications systems. No trust, no custom.

Privacy and data protection

Personal information is increasingly subject to regulation. There is international, foreign and industry-specific legislation and regulation. All OECD countries have some form of data protection and privacy legislation, and national regulations often overlap, are sometimes contradictory and almost all lack implementation guidance or adequate precision. Nevertheless, customers, staff, suppliers, tribunals and law courts all expect organisations to be proactive in their efforts to comply.

Originally very specific to the financial services industry, data protection regimes are spreading to all other industries. Technology – for communication, data sharing and data storage – will continue to evolve, creating new compliance challenges.

Privacy and data protection regulations vary from country to country; some are more lax, others more strict. Outsourcing is a potential source of risk, as data protection may be weaker in the outsource jurisdiction. The UK's Data Protection Act – in common with similar legislation across the EU – prohibits sending personal data outside the EEA except where suitable legislation ensures an adequate level of protection. New privacy legislation is proposed or is under way in many countries, including the EU and US. Around the world, companies that want to compete in the global economy will increasingly see privacy compliance as a basic 'cost of entry', rather like corporate governance.

Shareholders don't expect their companies to be in breach of national or international privacy regulations. Customers, staff and regulators are even fiercer. The ChoicePoint[1] and LexisNexis[2] cases should give every CEO sleepless nights: not only does dealing with the aftermath of the attack cost far more than installing appropriate measures in the first place, you still have to install them afterwards.

The consequences of failing to comply fully with data protection and privacy regulations are now so clear that we

---

[1] ChoicePoint, a US data broker registered in Georgia, was attacked by ID thieves who may have accessed 145,000 personal records; it has since then been subject to a US Federal Trade Commission enquiry into its compliance with the law, an SEC investigation into possible insider stock dealing and lawsuits in relation to both the Fair Credit Act and California state law.

[2] LexisNexis is a Reed Elsevier division that provides legal and business information; 310,000 individual subscription records may have been illegally accessed in 59 separate incidents over two years and, under various US laws, all had to receive letters and ongoing support from the company.

can't be far off the time when directors find themselves on the end of lawsuits for breach of fiduciary duty in respect of data protection and privacy regulation.

OECD Guidelines

The OECD Guidelines on privacy and data protection have become the international legal framework for data protection, both in the OECD (all of whose member states have adopted the guidelines) and in developing and transitional economies.

In 1990, the EU set about creating a framework that would bring the levels of data protection across the EU to a more common level. The EU's 1995 Data Protection Directive established a detailed privacy regulatory structure that EU member states have since then adopted into national law.

EU Regulation

EU Directives have been, and will continue to be, significant drivers of national regulation. The two most important EU instruments are the EU Data Protection Directive of 1995 (note that although the US was declared a 'safe harbor' for the purposes of EU data protection regimes in 2000 only a relatively small number of US companies fall within the 'safe harbor' arrangements) and the EU Directive on Privacy and Electronic Communications of 2002. In January 2012, the EU Commission released a draft European Data Protection Regulation, which will supersede the Data Protection Directive. It is expected that this will be finalised in 2014, with enforcement starting in 2016 following a transition period.

UK Regulation

Each country within the EU has incorporated the EU instruments into its national law. The UK's versions are identified below.

Data Protection Act 1998 (the 'DPA')

This act replaced the UK's 1984 Data Protection Act, which (among other defects) had failed to recognise the link between privacy and data protection. DPA requires any organisation that processes personal data to comply with eight enforceable principles of what it identifies as good practice.

The DPA (which is also interpreted in the light of the UK's Human Rights Act 2000) is concerned with personal data, and this encompasses facts and opinions about an individual and includes information about the data controller's intentions towards the individual (e.g. will s/he be employed or not?). Under the terms of the DPA, 'processing' includes storage, and the requirements apply to both electronic data and paper records (if they are contained in a 'relevant filing system'). The precise definitions of what is, and is not, covered have been further complicated by the findings of the 2003 Durant v Financial Services Authority court case and the Information Commissioner's updated guidance (on his website) is relevant.

The DPA covers a number of areas, including CCTV records, websites and Internet activity, recruitment and selection of staff, employment records, staff monitoring (including, for example, checking telephone records or Internet use) and information about workers' health.

Failure to comply with the DPA can result in substantial fines for organisations. The DPA creates something known as a section 55 criminal offence for individuals who, in specific circumstances, fail to comply. The DPA only applies if the data controller is established in the UK and/or the processing takes place in the UK; criminals based outside the EU and operating in breach of the DPA are able to do so with considerable impunity.

US Regulation

The Safe Harbor framework

This allows US companies that are regulated by the FTC and have operations in the EU to receive European personal data. They can comply with the EU Data Protection Directive by adopting the seven Safe Harbor Principles (the compliance standards are certified through the US Department of Commerce and enforced by the US Federal Trade Commission (FTC)) that are set out on the Commerce and FTC websites and submitting themselves to Commerce department certification.

The Gramm-Leach-Bliley Act ('GLBA')

The 'Financial Information Privacy Protection Act' was passed in 2001. It covers all US-regulated financial services companies, and charges their Boards with protecting their customers' personal information against any 'reasonably foreseeable' threats to their security, confidentiality or integrity. GLBA also applies to a wide range of 'non-bank' managers and the Federal Trade Commission (FTC), which is responsible for enforcing the Act, requires compliance with both the letter and spirit of the Act. GLBA requires directors to develop, draft, approve and implement an appropriate information security programme. Each organisation is required to determine its own best practice for achieving the objectives of GLBA and what official guidance there is, is inadequate.

The Fair Credit Reporting Act ('FRCA')

The FRCA was passed in 1999. It is designed to 'promote accuracy and ensure the privacy of the information used in credit reports', applies specifically to consumer reporting agencies (such as credit bureaus) and is enforced by the FTC. It is underpinned by a range of state laws.

The Health Insurance Portability and Accountability Act ('HIPAA')

This Act was passed in 1996 and took effect in April 2003. It requires healthcare organisations (health plans, doctors, hospitals, healthcare providers) to protect – and keep up to date – their patients' healthcare records (which includes patient account handling, billing and medical records), in order to streamline health industry inefficiencies, reduce paperwork, make the detection and prosecution of fraud easier, and to enable workers to more easily change jobs, even if they have pre-existing medical conditions. The 'Administrative Simplification (AS) Provisions' set out the security and privacy rules that institutions must implement in order to comply with HIPAA; these include rules for EDI, for electronic signatures and standards of privacy. Business partners are now also subject to the HIPAA requirements.

US State-level regulations

Starting with the Californian Senate Bill 1386 of 2003 (SB 1386), which requires any 'state agency or entity' holding personal information about customers living in California to divulge (which means press releases, communications to entire classes of customers and so on) any breaches of security for any databases that hold that personal information (unless the data is encrypted), State-level privacy regulation has spread across the US. SB 1386 was used as the template for similar privacy legislation in other states of the US; the 'unauthorised acquisition of computerised data that compromises the security, confidentiality, or integrity of personal information maintained by the person or business' triggers reputational damage for the data holder. Some states mandate compliance with PCI DSS regulations for e-commerce websites, and others mandate deployment of ISO27001 as guidance for state-level information security management systems.

APEC regulation

The 21 members of the Asia-Pacific Economic Cooperation forum endorsed, back in November 2004, a privacy framework that is primarily commercial in outlook. The framework is consistent with the OECD Guidelines and also emphasises the importance of privacy regimes in a region where many countries have not yet passed privacy protection laws. The framework adopts the EU and OECD definitions of personal information, and emphasises the benefits of participation in the global information economy; some countries (e.g. Australia) already have privacy and data-protection laws that are more in line with EU requirements than with those of APEC.

ISO27001

Throughout the OECD, and more recently in the APEC area, in the Americas and in many developing world countries, organisations are subject to a complex and often contradictory array of legislation and regulations related to information security – mostly related to data protection and individual privacy. ISO27001 helps organisations comply with these requirements – particularly in jurisdictions where data protection regulation is relatively new and there isn't an established body of case law and local good practice to fall back on. Deployment of the international Standard of best practice is always going to stand the board in good stead when faced with a data protection or privacy violation action of any sort.

Similarly, for organisations operating internationally across multiple jurisdictions and facing, therefore, complex compliance requirements, ISO27001 provides a structured and comprehensive method of minimising exposure to data protection and privacy violation actions in other parts of the world.

CHAPTER 12: ANTI-SPAM LEGISLATION

Executive summary

Unsolicited commercial e-mail is a threat to the availability of networks and information, because of the extent to which it can clog up the arteries of the Internet; it is also the subject of regulation. When it is carrying a payload (virus, spyware and so on) it can also be a threat to the confidentiality and integrity of that information. Organisations need to take action to defend themselves against spam and also to ensure that their own electronic marketing is not treated as spam.

Regulation of electronic marketing

One person's spam is another's useful e-mail marketing – and most companies are interested in e-mail marketing, at least at the level of regular newsletters and other updates, all of which could fall within the definition of spam. In the information age, as more and more marketing becomes digital (and Instant Messaging, mobile phones and VoIP become attractive marketing vectors), so more and more organisations will need to address the issue as part of their overall IT governance approach.

The EU Directive on Privacy and Electronic Communications was passed in July 2002, with a deadline for implementation of October 2003. It set out guidelines for how direct marketing should and should not be done. It placed obligations on the senders of unsolicited commercial e-mail, including the requirement that people be required to opt-in to receive unsolicited messages, that false sender identities and false return addresses should be prohibited and a genuine opt-out option should be provided.

UK Privacy and Electronic Communications Regulations 2003

For example, these UK regulations came into force on 11 December 2003 and superseded the earlier Telecommunications (Data Protection and Privacy) Regulations 1999. The UK's Information Commissioner is also responsible for enforcing these regulations.

The regulations cover use, by telecommunication network and service providers, and individuals, of any publicly available electronic communications network for direct marketing purposes, and any unsolicited direct marketing activity by telephone, fax, electronic mail (which includes text/video/picture messaging, SMS and e-mail) and by automated telephone calling systems. The key right conferred both on individuals and corporate entities is the right to register their objection to receiving unsolicited direct marketing material, and it provides a mechanism for doing this.

The detailed law around data protection and privacy is evolving as cases work their way through the courts.

US CAN-SPAM Act

The US CAN-SPAM Act ('Controlling the Assault of Non-Solicited Pornography and Marketing Act') of 2003 set national standards in the US for the sending of commercial e-mail and requires the Federal Trade Commission (FTC) to enforce its provisions. This Act permits e-mail marketers to send unsolicited commercial e-mail as long as it contains: an opt-out mechanism, a functioning return e-mail address, a valid subject line indicating it is an advertisement, and the legitimate physical address of the mailer. The bill includes many other provisions, such as the formation of a national do-not-spam list, and the prohibition of certain e-mail address collection methods. The 'do-not-spam' list idea was not a good one.

Many US states have also enacted anti-spam laws, some of which prohibit sending unsolicited commercial e-mail to state residents unless they have specifically opted-in to receive it.

Enforcement of legislation has been, in most jurisdictions, both weak and inconsistent. This is partly because enforcement is technologically difficult and partly because so much spam originates in jurisdictions beyond the control of any individual state.

The real anti-spam action, though, is really being taken by individual organisations. The most effective defences against spam are at the ISP level, the individual organisation's Internet gateway, and the individual user's anti-spam filters. These technological defences – which lead to the creation of 'black' and 'white' lists of e-mail marketers – are the key barriers now faced by any organisation attempting legitimately to use e-mail marketing as part of its marketing mix. And e-mail marketing works, but it only works for reputable companies if they comply with the law and apply best practice. Target customers have to trust you if they are going to put you on their e-mail marketing 'white list'.

ISO27001

The Standard provides guidance for effectively tackling the twin challenges of limiting the impact of incoming spam while ensuring that outgoing e-mail marketing is legal and appropriate.

CHAPTER 13: COMPUTER MISUSE LEGISLATION

Executive summary

Computer misuse legislation is relevant in two ways: authorities and organisations can take action under it against cyber criminals, and organisations have to ensure they comply with it themselves. Directors can be personally accountable for any compliance failures.

Convention on cyber crime

Computer crime legislation is relatively new. An OECD expert committee recommended, in 1983, that member countries ensure their penal legislation also applied to computer crime. The Council of Europe in 1989 adopted a recommendation from its own expert committee that identified the offences – which should be dealt with in computer-related legislation. Meanwhile, in 1990, the UK passed the Computer Crime Act and, in 2001, the Council of Europe adopted a Convention on Cybercrime that identified and defined Internet crimes, jurisdictional rights and criminal liabilities. The Convention, which came into force in 2005, identified the following types of crime:

- Offences against the confidentiality, integrity and availability of computer data and systems (illegal access, illegal interception, data interference, system interference, misuse of devices).
- Computer-related offences (computer-related forgery, computer-related fraud).
- Content-related offences (offences related to child

pornography).
- Offences related to infringements of copyright and related rights.

All organisations need to be aware of the Convention's provisions in article 12, paragraph 2: *'ensure that a legal person can be held liable where the lack of supervision or control by a natural person...has made possible the commission of a criminal offence established in accordance with this Convention'*. In other words, directors can be responsible for offences committed by their organisation simply because they failed to adequately exercise their duty of care. The Organization of American States (OAS) and APEC have both committed themselves to applying the European Convention on Cybercrime. More than 70 countries have enacted, or are in the process of enacting, computer crime laws, while 40 other countries have specifically ratified the European Convention on Cybercrime.

Computer Misuse Act 1990 ('CMA')

The UK's Computer Misuse Act 1990 was designed to set up provisions for securing computer material against unauthorised access or modification. It created three offences: the first is to knowingly use a computer to obtain unauthorised access to any program or data held in the computer; the second is to use this unauthorised access to commit one or more offences; the third is to carry out an unauthorised modification of any computer material. The Act allows for penalties in the form of both fines and imprisonment. This Act was updated by the Police and Justice Act of 2006, to broaden the range of potential cyber crimes in line with the experiences gained in investigating and prosecuting breaches of the Computer Misuse Act.

The Act basically outlaws, within the UK, hacking and the introduction of computer viruses. It hasn't been entirely successful in doing so. It initially had a significant impact on the computer policies of universities, often seen as the source of much of this sort of activity. It does have other implications for computer users in the UK. Anyone using someone else's username without proper authorisation is potentially committing an offence. Anyone copying data, who is not specifically authorised to do so, is potentially committing an offence. It also has relevance for organisations whose employees may be using organisational facilities to hack other sites or otherwise commit offences identified under the Act – not least because the source of any attack could be traced back to an organisational IP address.

The UK's All Party Internet Group (APIG) reviewed this Act in mid-2004 and recognised that it had been ineffective, largely through inadequate enforcement resourcing. It recommended a limited number of changes to CMA and a number of other actions, by other bodies, to improve the legal environment for computer security. While the amendments to the Act made in 2006 were clearly intended to make use of hacking tools illegal, it was equally possible to apply them to the use of legitimate tools that could be misused to conduct hacking activities.

ISO27001

As computer misuse legislation becomes more powerful, those organisations that have already taken effective action – through deployment of an ISO27001 Information Security

Management System – will be in a position where they are likely to be in line with the requirements of what are likely to be ill-aligned international laws.

CHAPTER 14: HUMAN RIGHTS

Executive summary

Human rights are an increasingly important issue in the information economy. They are, of course, important in every other sense as well; however, directors need to ensure that their organisational policies and procedures are compliant.

The UK's Human Rights Act 1998 ('HRA')

The HRA was enacted in October 2000. It incorporated into UK law the principles of the European Convention for the Protection of Human Rights and Fundamental Freedoms (the Convention). Most of the rights within the Convention are qualified, in that they are subject to limitations if the employer can show necessity to protect the rights and freedom of others. In particular, an employee could argue in a court or tribunal that the employer monitoring or tapping the employee's work telephone or e-mail or Internet activity was a breach of her/his rights under the Convention.

Regulation of Investigatory Powers Act 2000 ('RIPA')

Section 1 of the RIPA makes it unlawful to intentionally intercept communications over a public or private telecommunications network without lawful authority. Section 3 allows a defence if it can be reasonably believed that both parties consented to the interception. The Telecommunications (Lawful Business Practice) (Interception of Communications) Regulations 2000 (the Regulations) were issued under the powers of the RIPA and these allow employers to monitor employee communications where the employee has not given express consent, under only very specific conditions and for specified purposes.

Employers also have to take reasonable steps to inform employees that their communications might be intercepted. This means that employers must introduce Acceptable Use Policies that set out, for the employees, the right to monitor such communications.

ISO27001

Deployment of a best practice information security management system is likely to ensure that the organisation keeps in line with emerging Human Rights legislation around the world.

CHAPTER 15: RECORD RETENTION AND DESTRUCTION

Executive summary

Legislation, regulation, business contracts and prudence mandate the retention of specific records. These records are largely electronic (including e-mail) and their confidentiality and integrity needs to be protected throughout the period of retention, and they need to be accessible – in spite of intervening technology upgrades and system changes.

Records

An increasingly wide range of organisational and individual records (including e-mail, voice mail and Instant Message communications) must be retained to meet statutory or regulatory requirements, while others may be needed to provide adequate defence against potential civil or criminal action or to prove the (current and historic) financial status of the organisation to a range of potential interested parties, including shareholders, tax authorities and auditors, and to meet contractual liabilities. Records should be kept in a format that can prove they have not been tampered with, and so that they can be found many years later. This implies that organisations need an effective archive management policy and, inevitably, appropriate technology. Records do not (and should not) be kept for ever – this can make it difficult to find what is required as and when it is required, and the cost of storage is likely to be increasingly expensive.

Therefore, time limits – based, in each instance, on the maximum retention period identified in any of a statute of limitations, relevant legislation (including tax and company legislation) or specific regulatory requirements – should be set for the retention of each individual category of information. Information lifecycle management automates the process of moving information from primary (expensive) to secondary (much less expensive) storage devices. After the defined time period, records should be destroyed – in line with the procedure adopted by the organisation to ensure that any confidential information within those records is not inadvertently made public.

Failure to retain, in an accessible format (which might mean retaining versions of all old software and hardware after upgrades, in order to ensure accessibility) key records can have a significant impact on an organisation, not just in terms of fines and reputational impact, but also possibly in civil damages.

ISO27001

Application of appropriate controls, developed in line with the guidelines of the Standard, ensures both that data is retained and protected, and that the controls applied to protect retained information are consistent with those deployed for current information.

CHAPTER 16: INFORMATION SECURITY GOVERNANCE

Executive summary

The availability, integrity and confidentiality of its data are fundamental to the long-term survival of any 21st Century organisation. Unless the organisation takes a top down, comprehensive and systematic approach to protecting its information, it will be vulnerable to the wide range of threats identified in this book. These threats are a 'clear and present danger' to organisations of all sizes and in all sectors; responsibility for information risk management, for ensuring that the organisation appropriately defends its information assets, can no longer be abdicated or palmed off on the Head of IT. The Board has to take action. It's a part – and a very key part – of the Board's governance responsibility. Many (but not all) boards have shirked, or failed in this responsibility.

What is 'information security'?

'Information security', according to the internationally recognised overview of information security best practice, ISO/IEC 27000:2012, is defined as the 'preservation of confidentiality, integrity and availability of information.'

This book identifies the major information security issues facing boards and management teams and identifies how ISO27001, the International Standard of information security best practice, can give organisations a significant competitive and regulatory edge.

Information security is a Board responsibility

Information security is a governance issue, not solely an IT department functional responsibility. In an environment where it is not commercially sensible to invest in providing security against every possible risk, nor where 100 percent security is affordably achievable, there are five reasons for this:

1. The Board has to lay down guidelines as to which of the organisation's information assets are to be protected and the level to which this must be done.
2. The Board has to prioritise, and lay down guidelines for, investment in information security.
3. Information security is a 'whole business' exercise; effective information security requires a set of controls that integrate technology, procedure and human user behaviour in such a way that the Board's security objectives are achieved. Only the Board can set out the objectives and requirements for such a cross-organisational management system.
4. The whole organisation is at risk in the event of an information security breach (e.g. LexisNexis); corporate reputation, corporate earnings and corporate survival are the direct responsibility of the Board and the Board must, therefore, ensure that appropriate arrangements are made to protect the organisation from information risk.
5. It is the Board's direct responsibility to ensure that the organisation complies with the laws of the jurisdictions in which it trades. The growing body of information-related legislation is such that the Board now has to be proactive in mandating the implementation of a recognised information security

management system that will ensure compliance.

Governance and risk management

The Board's job is governance and strategy and, therefore, governing strategic and operational risk is a fundamental board responsibility. There are three operational risks (operational risk is 'the risk of direct or indirect loss resulting from inadequate or failed internal processes, people and systems or from external events'[1]) related to information and communications technology that boards need to consider:

1. Loss of proprietary information, with resultant damage to earning power and competitive position.
2. Loss of customer and personal data, with resultant damage to commercial and directors' personal reputations, as well as regulatory action, financial and punitive loss, and possible time in prison for directors.
3. Interruptions to business continuity, with resultant damage to commercial reputation and actual trading capability.

Boards have to prioritise the risks that are to be defended against in the light of the organisation's information assets, its business model and its overall business strategy. It has to ensure that appropriate resources are committed to realising and maintaining the risk profile that it has mandated.

---

[1] 'Operational Risk', a consultative document from the Basel Committee on Banking Supervision in January 2001.

Corporate governance codes

Corporate governance codes throughout the world recognise that the management of operational risk is a core board responsibility.

The UK's Combined Code requires listed companies to annually review *'all material controls, including financial, operational and compliance controls.'*[2] Internal Control: Guidance for Directors (previously known as the Turnbull Guidance) explicitly requires boards, on an ongoing basis, to identify, assess and deal with significant risks in all areas, including in *information and communications processes.*[3] Sarbanes-Oxley requires US-listed companies (and, increasingly, there is a knock-on effect on their major suppliers) to annually assess the effectiveness of their internal controls, and places a number of other significant governance burdens on executive officers, including the section 409 requirement that companies notify the SEC *'on a rapid and current basis such additional information concerning material changes in the financial condition or operations of the issuer.'* Pillar 1 of the Basel 2 Accord aims to reduce financial institutional *'exposures to the risk of losses caused by failures in systems, processes, or staff or that are caused by external events.'*[4]

Risk assessment has, over the last few years, become a pervasive and invasive concept: a risk assessment must be structured and formal, and nowadays one is expected in almost every context – from a school outing through to a

---

[2] Combined Code on Corporate Governance, Section C.2.1, September 2012.

[3] Internal Control: Guidance for Directors, paragraph 20, October 2005.

[4] BIS Press Release, 26 June 2004.

major corporate acquisition. It is certainly a cornerstone of today's corporate governance regimes. In the context of operational risk, a risk assessment is the first step that a board can take to controlling the risk; the most important step is the development of a risk treatment plan (in which risks are accepted, controlled, eliminated or contracted out) that is appropriate in the context of the company's strategic objectives.

Information risk

If no one else wanted it, it wouldn't be an asset. Information, to be useful to an organisation, must be available (to those who need to use it), confidential (so that competitors can't steal a march) and its integrity must be guaranteed (so that it can be relied upon). Information risk arises from the threats – originating both externally and internally – to the availability, confidentiality and integrity of the organisation's information assets.

Headline figures dramatically illustrate the cost of security failures. In 2005, the UK's National High Tech Crime Unit (NHTCU) reported[5] that 89 percent of firms interviewed had suffered some form of computer crime in the previous 12 months (up from 83 percent in the previous year), at a cost of at least £2.4bn, while the Detica report revealed that the cost had reached £27bn by 2011.

Threats to information security are wide ranging, complex and costly. External threats include casual criminals (virus

---

[5] 'Hi-Tech Crime: the Impact on UK Business 2005', survey conducted by NOP for the UK's NHTCU.

writers, hackers), organised crime (virus writers, hackers, spammers, fraudsters, espionage, ex-employees) and terrorists (including anarchists). More information security incidents (involving members of staff, contractors and consultants acting either maliciously or carelessly) originate inside the organisation than outside it. Baring, Enron, WorldCom and Lehman Brothers were all brought down by insiders. The indirect costs of these incidents usually far exceed their direct ones and the reputational impacts are usually even greater.

The need for determined action to deal with these risks should be self-evident.

Governance failure

The governance failure, though, is evident. An Ernst & Young survey[6] found that only 26 percent of organisations had assigned information security a CEO or COO level priority, and that only 42 percent said that their information security strategy was aligned to their business strategy. Ernst & Young summed it up: 'Information security needs to become a board-level priority and its executives need to have a seat at the boardroom table. And for a time, information security executives made great strides in achieving this level of visibility, accountability and value. But in recent years, as threats accelerate and economic volatility, emerging markets, offshoring and new

---

[6] Ernst & Young's 15th annual Global Information Security Survey, which interviewed 1,836 executives across 64 countries (*www.ey.com/Publication/vwLUAssets/Fighting_to_close_the_gap:_2012_G lobal_Information_Security_Survey/$FILE/2012_Global_Information_Secur ity_Survey___Fighting_to_close_the_gap.pdf*), November 2012.

technologies add complexity to the role, information security is having to compete with other board-level priorities. As a result, although information security is heading in the right direction, it may not be getting the attention it needs to keep pace with the velocity of change.

'An effective information security strategy needs to stretch across the entire enterprise and work in tandem with many different functional areas. That's why it is so important that information security's goals are aligned not only with the overall enterprise-wide business goals, but also with the various departmental and functional goals.'

In today's corporate governance environment, boards simply cannot afford to take their information security governance responsibilities anything less than seriously.

CHAPTER 17: BENEFITS OF AN ISO27001 ISMS

Executive summary

The benefits for an organisation in adopting and deploying an ISO27001 Information Security Management System are threefold:

1. Cost-effective, fit-for-purpose information security and regulatory compliance.
2. Out-performance vis-à-vis its competitors.
3. Competitive advantage.

A structured information security management system

Information security is a complex issue. Every information asset is subject to multiple threats and the interwoven mesh of related compliance regulation is such that there are no simple solutions. Information security has three key components: technological controls, procedural controls and user behaviour.

The Board has to prioritise its approach to information security and commit the investment and resources necessary to achieve its information security goals. It will need to commit certain sums to specific security technologies (anti-virus software, for instance), it will need to design and implement appropriate operational procedures (for updating and auditing anti-virus software deployments, for instance) and it will need to educate and train its staff (so they can tell the difference between a virus hoax and a real one, and know how they are required to respond to each, for instance).

A structured information security management system is based on an ongoing risk assessment process, identifying and classifying risk to organisational assets. It provides best practice guidance on the types of controls (which are procedural, technological and user-related) that might be appropriate for each risk, and provides guidance on implementation. It ensures that interrelationships between controls and control areas are plotted, so that potential conflicts can be resolved early.

Deploying a structured information security management system ensures that the organisation's information security management starting point is a comprehensive, integrated one with complete adaptability.

Benefits of a structured information security management system

'Almost 90% of the managers responded that the Standard had been adopted because it was recognised best practice in relation to information security. 80% also responded that the organisation had sought certification as a means of gaining competitive advantage within their respective markets.'[1]

'[O]ver a quarter of the organisations had sought certification because it was a condition of tenders, while in 16% of cases certification had been a mandatory requirement of a customer.'[2]

The benefits of adopting an externally certifiable

---

[1] ISO27001 Global Survey – Certification Europe, January 2008.
[2] Ibid

information security management system are, therefore, clear:

- The directors of the organisation will be able to demonstrate that they are complying with the requirements of Internal Control: Guidance for Directors (previously the Turnbull Guidance) and/or complying with current international best practice in risk management with regards to information assets and security.
- The organisation will be able to demonstrate, in the context of the array of data protection, privacy, computer misuse and anti-spam legislation, that is has taken appropriate action to comply with the laws.
- The organisation will be able to systematically protect itself from the dangers and potential costs of cyber attack, computer misuse, cyber crime and the impacts of cyber war.
- The organisation will be able to improve its credibility with staff, customers and partner organisations and this can have direct financial benefits through, for instance, improved sales.
- The organisation will be able to make informed, practical decisions about what security technologies and solutions to deploy and thus to increase the value for money it gets from information security, to manage and control the costs of information security and to measure and improve its return on its information security investments.

Boards that fail to tackle information security voluntarily are likely to find themselves forced to do it: 'Strong governance is the best indicator of senior leadership commitment to effective, consistent risk management across the organisation to achieve ongoing mission/business success.'[3]

Benefits of external certification ('registration') to ISO27001

There are a number of direct, practical reasons for implementing an information security policy and information security management system (ISMS) that is capable of being independently certified as compliant with ISO27001. A certificate tells existing and potential customers that the organisation has defined and put in place effective information security processes, thus helping create a trusting relationship.

A certification process also helps the organisation focus on continuously improving its information security processes. Of course, above all, certification, and the regular external review on which ongoing certification depends, ensures that the organisation keeps its information security system up to scratch and, therefore, that it continues to assure its ability to operate.

Most information systems are not designed from the outset to be secure. Technical security measures are limited in their ability to protect an information system. Management systems and procedural controls are essential components of any really secure information system and, to be effective, need careful planning and attention to detail.

ISO27001 provides the specification for an information security management system and, in the related Code of

---

[3] Managing Information Security Risk, published by the National Institute of Standards and Technology, March 2011.

Practice, ISO27002, it draws on the knowledge of a group of experienced information security practitioners in a wide range of significant organisations across more than 40 countries to set out best practice in information security. An ISO27001-compliant system will provide a systematic approach to identifying and combating the entire range of potential risks to the organisation's information assets. It will also provide directors of UK and US listed companies, of UK government organisations covered by the government's 'Orange Book' and directors in the supply chains of both public and private sector organisations, with both a systematic way of meeting their responsibilities under the Combined Code, the Turnbull Report and Sarbanes-Oxley, and the wide range of interlocking data protection and privacy legislation to which they are subject, and demonstrable evidence that they have done so to a consistent standard.

It also enables organisations outside the United Kingdom and United States to demonstrate that they are complying with their local corporate governance requirements as well as the data protection and privacy legislation in their local jurisdiction. Equally importantly, an ISO27001 certificate enables an organisation to demonstrate to any of its customers that its systems are secure; this, in the modern, global information economy, is at least as important as demonstrating compliance with local legislation. Possession of a suitably scoped ISO27001 certificate lets a supplier cost-effectively answer the information security and governance questions in request for proposal (RFP) and pre-tender questionnaires.

Certifying the organisation's ISMS to ISO27001 is a valuable step. It makes a clear statement to customers, suppliers, partners and authorities that the organisation has a secure information management system.

'Among the global drivers, is seeing certification based on ISO/IEC 27001 as establishing a common reference point for the certified company in the global market.'[4]

---

[4] ISO/IEC 27001 Information Systems Security Management Standard: Exploring the Reasons for Low Adoption, 2008.

CHAPTER 18: ISO27001 IN THE PUBLIC SECTOR

Executive summary

Many public-sector organisations usually face more significant threat levels than the private sector. All the threats identified earlier in this book apply, but in spades. In addition, many public-sector organisations are subject to very specific requirements in terms of information security structures.

UK public sector organisations

The OCSIA (Office of Cyber Security and Information Assurance) is the UK Government's Cabinet Office unit that is charged with working with the public and private sectors, and its international counterparts, to safeguard the UK's IT and telecommunications services. Specifically, the CSIA role is to provide a central, national focus for information security and its mission includes encouraging the private sector to develop a 'culture of security'. Its specific aims are to:

- Provide a strategic direction on cyber security and information assurance for the UK, including e-crime.
- Support education, awareness and training.
- Work with private-sector partners on exchanging information and promoting best practice.
- Ensure that the UK's information and cyber security technical capability and operational architecture is improved and maintained.
- Work with the Office of the Government Chief

Information Office (OGCIO) to ensure the resilience and security of government ICT infrastructures, such as the Public Sector Network (PSN) and G-cloud.

- Engage with international partners in improving the security of cyber space and information security.[1]

Government departments and other organisations involved in the protection of the UK's critical information infrastructure (finance, telecommunications, utilities, emergency services and so on) include:

- Centre for the Protection of National Infrastructure (CPNI)
- Serious Organised Crime Agency (SOCA)
- Home Office
- Department for Business, Innovation and Skills (BIS)
- Communications-Electronics Security Group (CESG)
- The Cabinet Office
- Office of Cyber Security and Information Assurance (OCSIA).

All UK central government departments are required to meet internationally recognised information security management standards (e.g. ISO27001) for their systems. The OCSIA has also produced and maintains security framework documents that provide key guidance for both central and local government on providing secure online services.

The OCSIA works with other government departments to maintain emergency telecommunications planning and business continuity plans. The OCSIA works with business

---

[1] *www.gov.uk/government/policy-teams/office-of-cyber-security-and-information-assurance*

to addresses the vulnerabilities of public sector and commercial telecommunications systems as well as those of the financial and banking sector.

The public sector collects and holds substantial quantities of data on a daily basis. Some of it is extremely sensitive and personal, and the government is required to protect its confidentiality. Patient health records, social service details, tax returns – all are held on information systems. Private sector organisations also handle personal data and are required to comply with legislation governing the protection of that information.

Government departments are also subject to the Data Protection Act, the Human Rights Act and the Freedom of Information Act. This means that government information systems must protect the information they handle and make the correct information available when required, and only for use by those people who are authorised to have access to it. The Ministry of Justice has published *Public Sector Data Sharing: Guidance on the Law.* (*See* www.justice.gov.uk).

The UK central government has rolled out a secure intranet, the Government Secure Intranet (GSI) Convergence Framework, for its telecommunications and e-mail services and Internet access. The GSI has been running since 1997, and was updated to the GSI Convergence Framework in 2011 to finalise the scope of the network. It imposes specific obligations on those organisations that wish to join it. It includes scope for local government and other government agencies to join, with the objective of 'creating a wider reaching, more secure and joined-up government service'.

The Cabinet Office requires central government departments to appoint a board-level Senior Information Risk Owner to be responsible for ensuring that departmental information security procedures are managed appropriately. This means that these procedures need to be based on (but not necessarily the same as – because there are specific central government versions of them) the controls of ISO27001.

The Office of the Deputy Prime Minister (ODPM) has encouraged local government to meet the same standards. Local authorities are now obliged to comply with ISO27001 as part of their regulatory obligations.

Freedom of information legislation

More than 90 countries around the world have passed some form of freedom of information legislation, which curtails government secrecy and requires specific categories of information to be made public in response to specific requests. Many other countries are reportedly working towards freedom of information legislation. Most countries have an information commissioner who is responsible for monitoring and enforcing the legislation. Usually, only public bodies are covered by such legislation and they can mostly be expected to be compliant with it. Certainly, public-sector organisations that defy freedom of information legislation can expect to be publicly pilloried and relentlessly pursued under the terms of the enabling legislation. Private companies, however, should note that one of the clear consequences of this type of legislation (the UK's Freedom of Information Act 2000 is a case in point) is that details of their previously confidential public sector tenders and contracts could now be made public, irrespective of any previous confidentiality clauses.

Board issues in the public sector

A key issue for public sector organisations is to find a balance between the bureaucracy of central government initiative implementation, the likelihood that the organisational Board will not have on it any individuals with current or meaningful information security experience, and the fact that central government is an even more enticing target for the world's wrong doers.

CHAPTER 19: IS ISO27001 FOR YOU?

Executive summary

Unless you're a tiny organisation (of say two or three people) or you do not use information or information technology inside the business, ISO27001 is an appropriate Standard for you to deploy to safeguard your IT infrastructure investments, protect your competitive position and ensure you comply with current and future national and international laws and regulations.

Do you have information that you rely on or which needs to be kept confidential?

If you do, you need to have a structured approach to protecting it against multiple external and internal threats. Such an approach requires a mix of technology and procedure, as well as informed and well-trained computer users. The Standard contains best practice guidelines on how to achieve this.

Do you collect personal information (e.g. from customers or employees)?

If you do, you need a structured approach to storing and protecting that information in a way that ensures your organisation is in compliance with a myriad of often conflicting international laws and regulations. The Standard contains best practice guidelines on how to achieve this.

Does your business rely on information technology for its daily activities?

If it does, you need a structured approach to ensuring that your systems continue operating without interruption and that your fall-back plans in case of disaster are thoroughly tested and dependable. The Standard contains best practice guidelines on how to achieve this.

Do your customers, suppliers or partners need confidence in your information handling and privacy protection measures?

External certification of your information security management system can provide customers, partners and suppliers with the confidence to move forward in dealing with you, knowing that you maintain secure information systems.

Can you afford reputational damage, commercial and punitive losses, business interruption and loss or corruption of confidential information?

Probably not.

If your answers to the first four questions are 'Yes' and to the last is 'No', then you need to deploy a structured information security management system, and as soon as possible. The question that remains is: 'Is ISO27001 the answer?'

Is ISO27001 the answer?

The answer depends on the size and complexity of the

organisation, and the commercial drivers. In practical terms, if you employ fewer than five people, ISO27001 is only likely to be appropriate if there are specific commercial reasons for pursuing it: if you operate in a high-risk environment (e.g. financial services), if there is a customer requirement (e.g. service desk outsourcing services) or if there is some other mandate (e.g. government or funding requirements).

CHAPTER 20: HOW DO YOU GO ABOUT ISO27001?

Once the Board has recognised the need to deploy a structured information security management system, the steps to implementation are relatively straightforward. There are three preparatory steps that should be taken in every instance.

Preparation

The first is to obtain, and study, copies of both ISO27001 and ISO27002. It is against these Standards specifically that compliance will be measured and they, therefore, have precedence over any other guidance or commentary. Copies of the Standards can be obtained from your national standards body or from *www.itgovernance.co.uk* (IT Governance Ltd is an authorised BSI international distributor).

The second is to obtain, and study, detailed guidance on how to take the project forward. One of the best available manuals that fulfils this function is *IT Governance: An International Guide to Data Security and ISO27001/ISO27002*, (5th edition), which is available from *www.itgovernance.co.uk*, from Amazon, or from most good bookshops.

Thirdly, you need to determine whether or not your ISO27001 system is to fit in with any other management system (e.g. ISO9001) and take appropriate steps to map ISO27001 components to your existing management system.

Initial planning

The first planning step is to identify all the stakeholders relevant to your ISMS and what their requirements are, including legal and regulatory requirements, and contractual obligations. This should also include the organisation's specific needs and obligations.

Following this, you will need to conduct a scoping exercise to determine exactly which parts of the organisation should be within the scope of the ISMS, and which not. In larger, more complex organisations, there may be benefits in a staged approach to implementation. Scoping is usually the first part of the initial gap analysis.

Next, you need to carry out an initial gap analysis, to identify the gap between your existing information security system and the specification contained in ISO27001. This initial gap analysis is carried out at a high level; its primary objective is to inform your ISO27001 project plan.

Policy drafting, project planning and securing ongoing board commitment are also essential. Without detailed planning and real board commitment, your project will not deliver the expected benefits and will, ultimately, fail.

Implementation

Once the Board is committed, the key project stages are below (and are outlined in substantially more detail in *Nine Steps to Success: An ISO27001:2013 Implementation overview*, available online from IT Governance):

- A risk analysis and risk assessment, which (if appropriate) is integrated into any existing

risk-management frameworks or methodologies you
may have. A risk assessment is a systematic
consideration of:

1. The business harm likely to result to each
   identified information asset from a range of
   specific, possible business failures.
2. The realistic likelihood of each such failure
   occurring.

- Identification of the treatment and controls that are
  appropriate for each of the identified risks (what
  ISO27001 calls a Statement of Applicability).
- Generation of the policies, procedures and work
  instructions that are necessary to document your ISMS,
  and their integration into any other management system
  you already have in place. This is the most
  time-consuming aspect of your ISO27001 project and
  you should deploy pre-written policy, procedure and
  work instruction templates (for instance, the *ISO27001:
  2013 ISMS Documentation Toolkit* – available via
  download or CD-ROM) to help you cost-effectively
  accelerate and fast track this process.
- An operational implementation plan, to bring the
  infrastructure, processes and competences up to the
  required standard. This plan may contain a number of
  individual security improvement programmes that
  tackle specific areas of weakness in greater depth.
- A communication and training plan, to ensure that all
  users of the IT systems work within the improved
  information security environment; this should be
  effectively integrated into your existing HR and
  training framework and activities. Purchasing and
  deploying multiple copies of this book can
  substantially assist in the process of getting

organisation-wide understanding of the need for an ISMS and the consequent 'buy in' to the project.
- Internal compliance audit programme, to check that each control area has been effectively implemented, to identify and implement possible improvements, and to prepare for certification.
- Selection of external certification organisations and actual certification.

CHAPTER 21: SELECTION OF A CERTIFICATION BODY

Any organisation seeking accredited certification will want to be sure that there is a cultural fit between itself and its supplier of certification services, and there will certainly be all the normal issues of ensuring that there is alignment between the desires of the buyer and the vendor's offering, including pricing and service. It is completely appropriate to treat the selection of a certification body with the same professionalism as the selection of any other supplier.

There are three key issues that do need to be taken into account when making this selection: the first is generic, the second is relevant to organisations that already have one or more externally certified management systems in place, and the third applies specifically to organisations tackling ISO27001.

You should always use an accredited certification body (CB). Each country has its own national accreditation body (UKAS in the UK), and the Accreditation Body is responsible for ensuring that Certification Bodies are capable of assessing and certifying organisations against specific international standards, and for also ensuring that all accredited certificates are internationally recognised and accepted.

It is essential that your ISMS is fully integrated into your organisation: it will not work effectively if it is a separate management system and exists outside of and parallel to any other management systems. Logically, this means that the framework, processes and controls of the ISMS must, to the greatest extent possible, be integrated with, for instance, your ISO9001 quality system; you want one document control system, you want one set of processes for each part of the organisation and so on. Clearly, therefore, assessment of your management systems must also be integrated: you only want one audit, which deals with all the aspects of your management system. It is simply too disruptive of the organisation, too costly and too destructive of good business practice to do anything else. You should take this into account when selecting your ISO27001 certification body, and ensure that whoever you choose can and does offer an integrated assessment service.

The second issue that you should take into account when selecting your supplier of certification services is their approach to certification itself. An ISMS is fundamentally designed to reflect the organisation's assessment of risks in and around information security. In other words, each ISMS will be different. It is important, therefore, that each external assessment of an ISMS takes that difference into account so that the client gets an assessment that *adds value* to its business, rather than one that is merely a mechanical comparison of the ISMS against the requirements of ISO27001.

In the UK, the United Kingdom Accreditation Service (UKAS) operates under a Memorandum of Understanding from the Department for Business, Innovation and Skills. UKAS accredits the competence of certification bodies – both inside and outside the UK – to perform services in the areas of product and management system approval.

As described earlier, the organisation should use only an accredited certification body when seeking ISO27001 certification. A list of organisations that have achieved ISO27001 certification, together with the scope of each certificate, can be reviewed at the website of the international user group: *www.iso27001certificates.com*. A certificate is usually valid for up to three years.

APPENDIX: ISO27001 – PAST, PRESENT AND FUTURE

ISO27001 was originally published at BS 7799, which was the outcome of a joint initiative by the DTI (now the Department for Business, Innovation and Skills) in the UK and leading UK private sector businesses. The working party, which started work in 1992, produced the first version of BS 7799 in February 1995. This was originally a Code of Practice for IT Security Management. Organisations that developed ISMSs that complied with this Code of Practice were able to have them independently inspected, but there was initially no UKAS scheme in place and, therefore, formal certification was not possible. An alternative solution, known as 'c:cure', was adopted to provide a framework for implementation of the Standard, and was available from April 1997. The confusion around c:cure and the absence of UKAS accredited certification resulted in a slower-than-anticipated uptake of certification to the Standard. c:cure was effectively withdrawn as an option late in 2000.

BS 7799 underwent a significant review in 1998. Feedback was collated and, in April 1999, a revised Standard was launched. The original Code of Practice was significantly revised and retained as Part 1 of the British Standard and a new Part 2 was added. Part 1 was re-titled 'Code of Practice for Information Security Management' and provided guidance on best practice in information security management. Part 2, titled 'Specification for Information Security Management Systems', formed the Standard against which an organisation's security management system was to be assessed and certified.

BS 7799-2 underwent a further review during 2002 and a number of significant changes were made. BS 7799-2 formed 'the basis for an assessment of the Information Security Management System (ISMS) of the whole, or part, of an organisation. It [could] be used as the basis for a formal certification scheme'. It was, in other words, the specific document against which an ISMS was assessed. The 2005 revision of ISO/IEC 17799 (*see below*) led to a change in the controls that was reflected in the new international version of the Standard, ISO27001.

As a Code of Practice, BS 7799-1 took the form of guidance and recommendations. Its foreword clearly stated that it was not to be treated as a specification. It became internationalised as ISO/IEC 17799 in December 2000. BS 7799-2, on the other hand, was internationalised as ISO/IEC 27001:2005.

ISO/IEC 17799

In 1998, when the original BS 7799 was revised for the first time, prior to becoming BS 7799-1, references to UK legislation were removed and the text was made more general. It was also made consistent with OECD guidelines on privacy, information security and cryptography. Its best practice controls were made capable of implementation in a variety of legal and cultural environments.

In 2000, BS 7799–1:1999 was, as indicated above, submitted as the proposed text of an international standard and was re-issued with minor changes as BS ISO/IEC 17799:2000. In the UK, it also had the dual number BS 7799–1:2000. It was issued as a single-part Standard, titled

'Information Technology – Code of Practice for Information Security Management', and replaced BS 7799–1:1999, which was then withdrawn. BS 7799–2:1999 was then replaced by the 2002 version and this, in turn, was replaced with ISO/IEC 27002:2005 and, eventually, in the updated ISO/IEC 27002:2013 alongside ISO/IEC 27001:2013. With the revised Annex A, it is the Standard against which an ISMS is certified.

The reason for developing an international Standard on information security management was described by BSI, on its website, as follows: 'many organizations have expressed the need to have a common standard on best practice for information security management. They would like to be able to implement information security controls to meet their own business requirements as well as a set of controls for their business relationships with other organizations. These organizations see the need to share the benefits of common best practice at a true international level to ensure that they can protect their business processes and activities to satisfy these business needs.'

In other words, the ISO 27002:2013 Code of Practice is intended to provide a framework for international best practice in Information Security Management and systems interoperability. It also provides guidance, to which an external auditor will look, on how to implement a certifiable ISMS. It does NOT, as the Standard is currently written, provide the basis for an international certification scheme.

Links to other standards and regulatory frameworks

ISO27001 was designed to harmonise with ISO 9001:2008

and ISO 14001:2004 so that management systems can be effectively integrated. It can be readily implemented with the Plan-Do-Check-Act (PDCA) model and reflects the principles of the 2002 OECD guidance on the security of information systems and networks.

ISO27001 implicitly recognises that information security and any Information Security Management System (ISMS) should form an integrated part of any internal control system created as part of Corporate Governance procedures and that the Standard fits in with the approach adopted by the Turnbull Committee.

USEFUL WEBSITES

IT Governance Ltd (the company)
www.itgovernance.co.uk

Blogspot
www.alancalderitgovernanceblog.com

ISO27001 certification organisations

United Kingdom Accreditation Service
www.ukas.com

BSI
www.bsigroup.com

Bureau Veritas Quality International (BVQI)
www.bureauveritas.com

DNV Certification Ltd
www.dnv.com

Lloyd's Register Quality Assurance Ltd (LRQA)
www.lrqa.com

National Quality Assurance Ltd (NQA)
www.nqa.com

SGS Yarsley
www.sgs.com

Governance

(US) Corporate Governance
www.corpgov.net

(UK) Department for Business, Innovation and Skills
www.gov.uk/government/organisations/department-for-business-innovation-skills

European Corporate Governance Institute
www.ecgi.org/index.htm

Internet Watch Foundation
www.iwf.org.uk

National Association of Corporate Directors
www.nacdonline.org

(UK) Government Procurement Service
http://gps.cabinetoffice.gov.uk/

Project Management Institute
www.pmi.org

Information security

(UK) Alliance Against IP Theft
www.allianceagainstiptheft.co.uk

Anti-phishing Working Group
www.antiphishing.org

(UK) Communications – Electronics Security Group
www.cesg.gov.uk

Carnegie Mellon Software Engineering Institute Computer
Emergency Response Team (CERT) Coordination Centre
www.cert.org

Computer Security Institute
www.gocsi.com

Computer Security Resource Clearinghouse (US National
Institute of Standards and Technology)
http://csrc.nist.gov

(US) US Computer Emergency Readiness Team
www.us-cert.gov

(UK) Federation Against Software Theft
www.fastiis.org

Forum of Incident Response and Security Teams
www.first.org

GCHQ
www.gchq.gov.uk

(US) Government Accountability Office
www.gao.gov

Information Commissioner
www.ico.org.uk

ISO27001 User Group
www.iso27001usergroup.co.uk

Information Systems Audit and Control Association
www.isaca.org

Information Systems Security Association
www.issa.org

Institute for Internal Auditors
na.theiia.org

Internet Security Alliance
www.isalliance.org

(UK) Centre for the Protection of the National Infrastructure (CPNI)
www.cpni.gov.uk

(US) National Infrastructure Coordinating Center
www.dhs.gov/national-infrastructure-coordinating-center

The SANS Institute
www.sans.org

(UK) Intellectual Property Office
www.ipo.gov.uk

ITG RESOURCES

IT Governance Ltd sources, creates and delivers products and services to meet the real-world, evolving IT governance needs of today's organisations, directors, managers and practitioners.

The ITG website (*www.itgovernance.co.uk*) is the international one-stop-shop for corporate and IT governance information, advice, guidance, books, tools, training and consultancy.

www.itgovernance.co.uk/iso27001.aspx is the information page on our website for ISO27001 resources.

Other Websites

Books and tools published by IT Governance Publishing (ITGP) are available from all business booksellers and are also immediately available from the following websites:

www.itgovernance.eu is our euro-denominated website, which ships from Benelux and has a growing range of books in European languages other than English.

www.itgovernanceusa.com is a US$-based website that delivers the full range of IT Governance products to North America, and ships from within the continental US.

www.itgovernance.in provides a selected range of ITGP products specifically for customers in the Indian sub-continent.

www.itgovernance.asia delivers the full range of ITGP publications, serving countries across Asia Pacific. Shipping from Hong Kong, US dollars, Singapore dollars, Hong Kong dollars, New Zealand dollars and Thai baht are all accepted through the website.

Toolkits

ITG's unique range of toolkits includes the IT Governance Framework Toolkit, which contains all the tools and guidance that you will need in order to develop and implement an appropriate IT governance framework for your organisation.

For a free paper on how to use the proprietary Calder-Moir IT Governance Framework, and for a free trial version of the toolkit, see *www.itgovernance.co.uk/calder_moir.aspx*.

There is also a wide range of toolkits to simplify implementation of management systems, such as an ISO/IEC 27001 ISMS or an ISO/IEC 22301 BCMS, and these can all be viewed and purchased online at *www.itgovernance.co.uk*.

Training Services

IT Governance offers an extensive portfolio of training courses designed to educate information security, IT governance, risk management and compliance professionals. Our classroom and online training programmes will help you develop the skills required to deliver best practice and compliance to your organisation. They will also enhance your career by providing you with industry standard certifications and increased peer recognition. Our range of courses offer a structured learning path from Foundation to Advanced level in the key topics of information security, IT governance, business continuity and service management.

ISO/IEC 27001:2013 is the international management Standard that helps businesses and organisations throughout the world develop a best-in-class Information Security Management System. Knowledge and experience in implementing and maintaining ISO27001 compliance are considered to be essential to building a successful career in information security. We have the world's first programme of certificated ISO27001 education with Foundation, Lead Implementer, Risk Management and Lead Auditor training courses. Each course is designed to provide delegates with relevant knowledge and skills and an industry-recognised qualification awarded by the International Board for IT Governance Qualifications (IBITGQ).

Full details of all IT Governance training courses can be found at *www.itgovernance.co.uk/training.aspx*.

Professional Services and Consultancy

Your mission to plug critical security gaps will be greatly assisted by IT Governance consultants, who have advised hundreds of information security managers in the adoption of ISO27001 Information Security Management Systems (ISMS).

The organisation's assets, security and data systems, not to mention its reputation, are all in your hands. A major security breach could spell disaster. Timely advice and support from IT governance experts in tackling ISO27001 will enable you to identify the threats, assess risks and put in place the necessary controls before there's an incident.

At IT Governance, we understand that information, information security and information technology are always business issues, and not just IT ones. Our consultancy services assist you in managing information security strategies in harmony with business goals, conveying the right messages to your colleagues to support decision making.

For more information about IT Governance Consultancy, see: *www.itgovernance.co.uk/consulting.aspx*.

Publishing Services

IT Governance Publishing (ITGP) is the world's leading IT-GRC publishing imprint that is wholly owned by IT Governance Ltd.

With books and tools covering all IT governance, risk and compliance frameworks, we are the publisher of choice for authors and distributors alike, producing unique and practical publications of the highest quality, in the latest formats available, which readers will find invaluable.

www.itgovernancepublishing.co.uk is the website dedicated to ITGP enabling both current and future authors, distributors, readers and other interested parties to have easier access to more information. This allows ITGP website visitors to keep up to date with the latest publications and news.

Newsletter

IT governance is one of the hottest topics in business today, not least because it is also the fastest moving.

You can stay up to date with the latest developments across the whole spectrum of IT governance subject matter, including: risk management, information security, ITIL® and IT service management, project governance, compliance and so much more, by subscribing to ITG's core publications and topic alert e-mails.

Simply visit our subscription centre and select your preferences: *www.itgovernance.co.uk/newsletter.aspx*.

Lightning Source UK Ltd.
Milton Keynes UK
UKHW021042050619
343916UK00012B/1315/P